No matter how modern a city is, some
wildlife is bound to come and live
in it. Man must share the earth with
other creatures.

ROBIN

Larger mammals do not often come
into the city. They are too fearful
of man. But sometimes you will hear
about a fox or a deer or even a bear
that wanders into the city by mistake.

GRAY FOX

OPOSSUM

Opossums are slow-witted mammals
that are more common in cities than
many people suppose. They creep
about only at night, eating garbage.

Sometimes man's tamed animals go wild. Hardly any wild dogs live in our cities today; but there are thousands of cats making a living on their own as true "wildlife."

COTTONTAIL RABBIT

The cottontail rabbit is a common animal
of parks and yards. It eats plants
and likes to bite off tender sprouts of
flowers and vegetables.

Shyer still is the small "flying" squirrel — which really glides rather than flies. It is quite common but comes out only at night, hunting insects and plant food.

FLYING SQUIRREL

Fox squirrels live on the edges of
the city. They are larger and shyer
than their gray cousins.

FOX SQUIRREL

GRAY SQUIRREL

Gray squirrels, very common in some
city parks, store acorns for the winter.
They are active all year when the
weather is good.

COTTONTAIL RABBIT

When snow covers the city, you may find
tracks of mammals. You may be surprised
to see how many are about — although some
are active only at night.

OPOSSUM

RAT

CAT

MALLARD

Some kinds of ducks may raise a family in city ponds and stay all year 'round if the water does not freeze.

BLACK DUCK

PINTAIL

Large water birds, just passing through the city, stop for food at park lakes. They are often seen in the autumn, as they go south for the winter.

GREAT BLUE HERON

EGRET

CANADA GOOSE

MUSEUM OF SCIENCE

LARGEMOUTH BASS

SNAPPING TURTLE

Fishes are eaten by larger fishes —
and by snapping turtles and water
snakes, too. Many children enjoy
fishing in city ponds.

Fish swim down rivers to the city and may stay because they find food. But waste matter from city sewers and factories often pollutes the water and kills the fish.

CATFISH

CARP

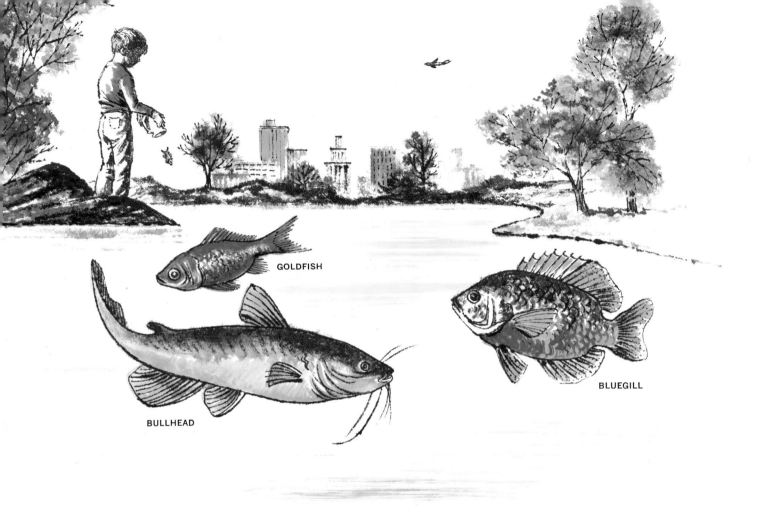

GOLDFISH

BULLHEAD

BLUEGILL

Tiny pond animals are food for fish.
Most city ponds and lakes are stocked
with fish by man. Children may let
their pet goldfish go into ponds, too.

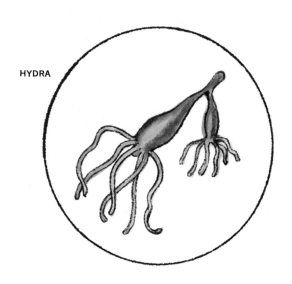

HYDRA

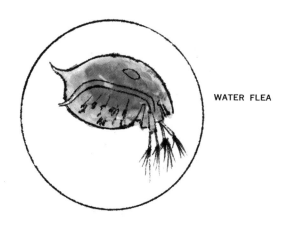

WATER FLEA

The waters of a pond are home to many
tiny creatures that can best be seen
with a magnifying glass. Mosquitos lay
their eggs in any standing water.

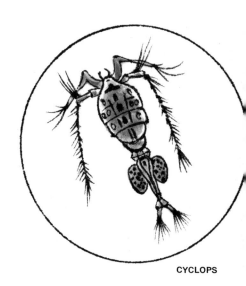

CYCLOPS

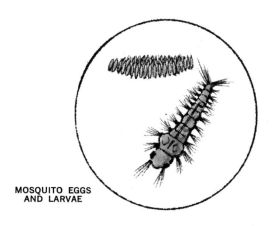

MOSQUITO EGGS
AND LARVAE

TREE FROG

Green frogs and leopard frogs may
live at the water's edge. And in weeds
and trees nearby there may be tree frogs
and spring peepers.

LEOPARD FROG

City parks often have ponds or rivers.
Wherever there is water, you are likely
to find many kinds of animals. Around
the shore there may be toads, salamanders,
and perhaps turtles.

PAINTED TURTLE

DUSKY SALAMANDER

AMERICAN TOAD

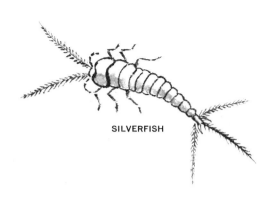

SILVERFISH

Here are other insect pests sometimes found in city houses.

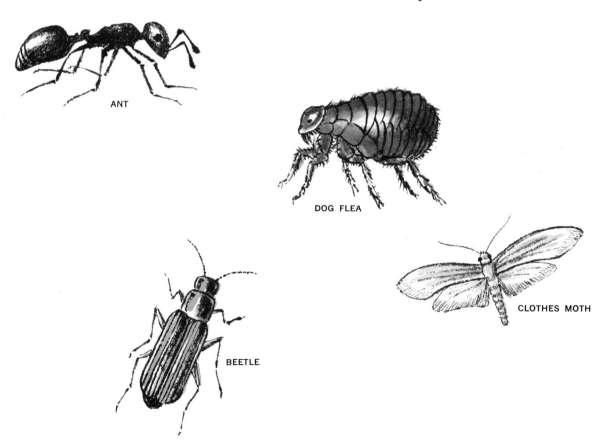

ANT

DOG FLEA

BEETLE

CLOTHES MOTH

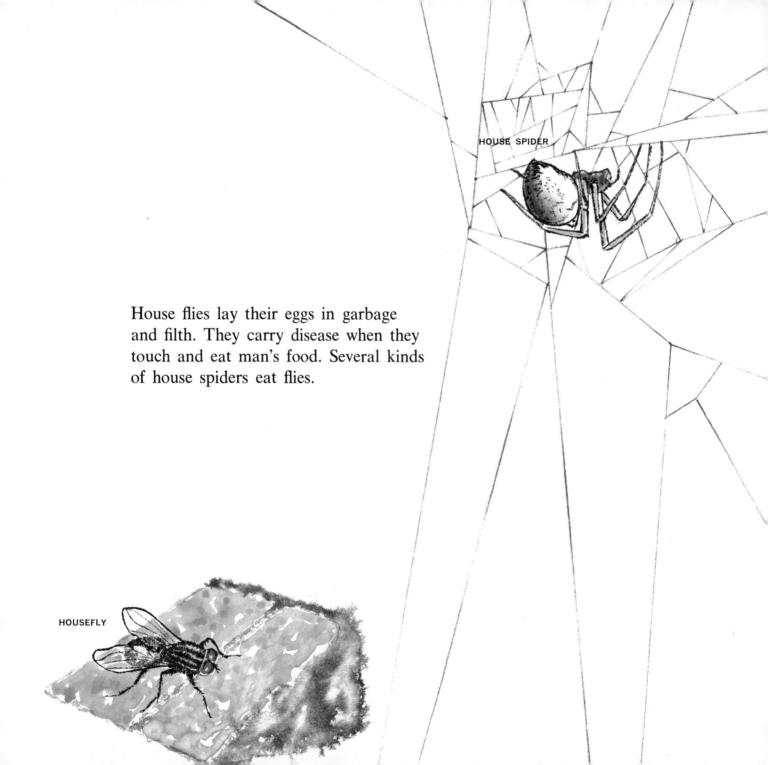

HOUSE SPIDER

House flies lay their eggs in garbage and filth. They carry disease when they touch and eat man's food. Several kinds of house spiders eat flies.

HOUSEFLY

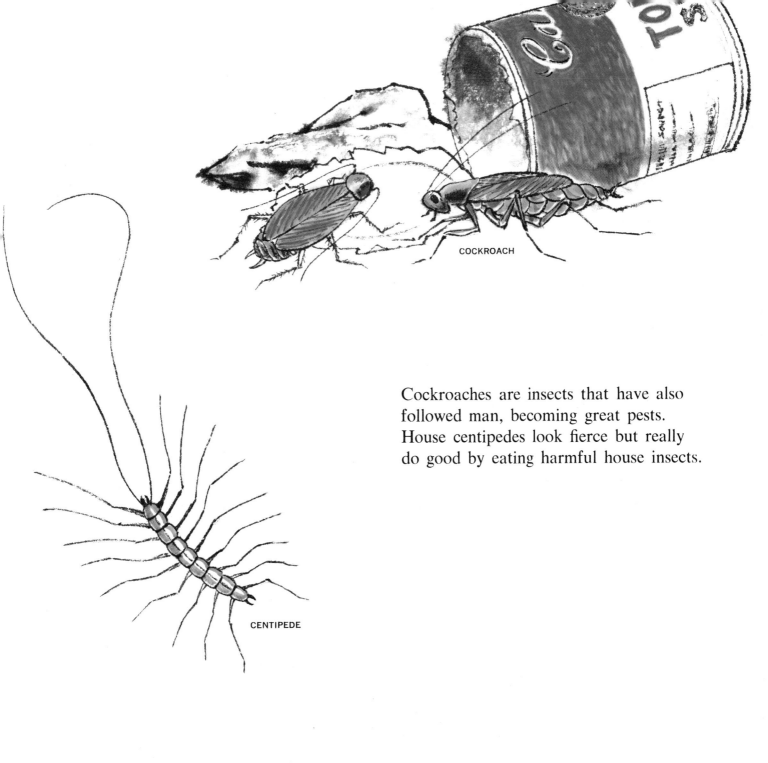

COCKROACH

CENTIPEDE

Cockroaches are insects that have also
followed man, becoming great pests.
House centipedes look fierce but really
do good by eating harmful house insects.

HOUSE MOUSE

The real house mouse seldom goes outside.
It is an animal that has followed man
all over the world. The more harmful
Norway rat also lives in buildings and
eats man's food.

NORWAY RAT

SCREECH OWL

Mouselike animals you may see outdoors are usually the tiny plant-eaters called voles. They are active at night, when small owls may hunt them.

MEADOW VOLE

Wherever lawns and flowers are planted,
insects and earthworms will come to live.
Moles and shrews are small animals that
may feed on ground-dwelling creatures.

PEREGRINE FALCON

English sparrows and pigeons eat
weed seeds and food dropped by
people. Sometimes these birds are
hunted by falcons which make their
nests on tall buildings.

CITY PIGEON

CHIMNEY SWIFT

During the day, insects are hunted
by chimney-swifts, starlings, robins,
purple martins, and cardinals. All
of these birds can live in the city.

ROBIN

STARLING

CARDINAL

PURPLE MARTIN

Another insect-eater, the nighthawk, cries *peent* as it flies. This bird lays its eggs on flat roofs.

NIGHTHAWK

LITTLE BROWN BAT

LEOPARD MOTH

Bats are flying mammals that hunt
insects at night and spend their days
hiding and sleeping around the tops of
buildings.

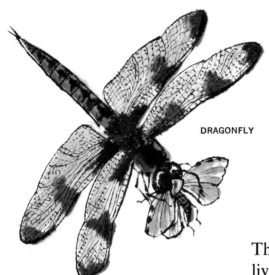

DRAGONFLY

There are many other kinds of insects living in the city. They are food for other creatures. Some of the hunters are insects, too.

CICADA-KILLER WASP

On a summer night in the city, you
can often hear the singing of crickets,
cicadas, and katydids. And fireflies
blink in grassy places.

FIREFLY

KATYDID

CRICKET

Hawkmoths may fly to apartment window boxes. Large silkworm moths make cocoons that can be found on shrubs in winter.

FIVE-SPOTTED HAWKMOTH

COMMON SULPHUR

PAINTED LADY

RED ADMIRAL

TIGER SWALLOWTAIL

QUESTION MARK

These are some butterflies you may see in the city.

Some caterpillars, the young of moths and butterflies, may eat so much that they become pests. Others feed mainly on weeds.

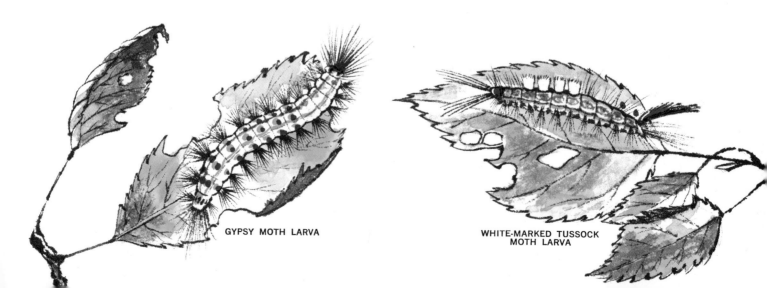

GYPSY MOTH LARVA

WHITE-MARKED TUSSOCK MOTH LARVA

ADULT MOTH

MAPLE SPANWORM
LARVA

Flying creatures enter the city very easily. But they will not stay unless they can find food and a good place to live. Many winged insects lay their eggs on trees and plants in the city.

Cities are made by man, for man to
live in. People bring some plants
and animals along with them. But
others come by themselves — and these
are the creatures called wildlife.

WILDLIFE
IN THE CITY

JULIAN MAY

illustrated by BILL BARSS

CREATIVE EDUCATIONAL SOCIETY, INC.
MANKATO, MINNESOTA 56001